Liquids

Fluid ozs	UK pints	US pints	US cups	Millilitres	Or
1				29	
16		1	2	473.6	475
20	1			568.3	570

Herbs

Meat: Basil, Lovage, Oregano, Rosemary, Sage, Thyme, Savory

Poultry: Chervil, Tarragon, Burnet, Lemon Grass, Savory

Fish: Basil, Bay, Chervil, Coriander, Dill, Tarragon, Thyme, Burnet, Lemon Grass, Savory, Fennel, Parsley

Soups & stews: Basil, Bay, Chervil, Coriander, Lovage, Marjoram, Rosemary, Tarragon, Savory

Salads: Basil, Chervil, Chives, Dill, Lovage, Mint, Rosemary, Sage, Tarragon, Bergamot, Tansy, Sorrel, Parsley

Sauces: Rosemary, Tarragon, Thyme, Mint, Parsley

Eggs: Basil, Chervil, Chives, Tarragon, Lemon Balm, Savory, Tansy

Pasta: Basil, Rosemary, Hyssop, Oregano, Marjoram

Cooking Basics

Cooking Basics

Parsimony Press
2000

ACKNOWLEDGMENTS

Acknowledgments are due to the numerous people who cook on
television, who write about cooking, who don't write about cooking,
who complain about tools and the many others who believe that
everybody else is wrong, and only they know best.

Particular thanks are due to Lucy Image whose cooking for pop
musicians has given the wisdom of experience to her advice.

First Published in Great Britain in 2000
Second Impression 2000
Parsimony Press Limited
West Huntspill, Somerset

A CIP catalogue record for this book is available from the British Library

ISBN 1 902979 04 4

Editor: Robert Norton
Typeset and Design: Eiichi Kono
Photography: Ian Thraves and Robert Norton
Printed and bound by: Poligrafico Dehoniano, Italy

Contents

Introduction

There is more written about cooking than most of us can ever read. The trouble is that a lot of it either sells one person's view about how a job should be done, or – perhaps even and – assumes that the reader knows the things that are not explained.

To some extent we hope our little book will overcome this problem. Our other editions will go into things more thoroughly, such as more about kitchen tools, or a whole book on what you might like to know about potatoes, or soups, or handling fish.

But here we are dealing with the real essentials, and filling it out with a few other thoughts, less essential, but worth knowing.

The most important ingredient in all cooking, by far, is love. There are very few ways that we can give to each other in life that are better than making something with our own hands to give to another. In cooking this can even be a soft boiled egg for somebody ill in bed. Simplicity doesn't matter. It is, I believe, even an advantage.

When cooking becomes a complicated exercise that takes over the kitchen and sometimes even the house, it is not so much a giving as an exercise in vanity. 'Look at me, I'm a great chef, and you had better be grateful when you sit down to eat what I have made.'

A while back, on television, I watched Raymond Blanc cooking, for Sophie Grigson, a vegetable soup that his mother used to make. It took only a few minutes. There were no expensive ingredients. Yet it was the dish I would most like to have eaten of all those that he makes, because it was as lovingly made as any dish can be. There was a tenderness about the process as he made it, clearly remembering his mother, and thinking about how much of each ingredient to use. How carefully he chose them, how lovingly he cooked them. It would have been an honour to be given a bowl.

Please start with this in mind. The more you cook, the more you will want to try new things, and the more sophisticated your cooking may become. This is fine. But do not let it all become, as some people do, an exercise in having the tail wag the dog. The end result *must* be a loving gift, something to be eaten with pleasure. Who cares what it looks like if it tastes dull? Who cares what it tastes like if the real reason for it was to earn the cook more praise than somebody else who cooks?

Please therefore start with the certain knowledge that if you can only scramble eggs lovingly you are already a better cook than somebody who can make a seven course meal without love.

What you start with

You need at least two knives. One is large and fairly hefty, and is used for cutting anything from a melon to a piece of beef. It is also used for chopping.

The other is smaller, and is used for all the little burrowing kind of cutting, whether it be removing the beaks of squids, or opening a mango, or cutting the stems out of the leaves of spring greens.

You need something to sharpen these knives. The most expensive knife you can buy, and there are plenty of them about, is useless if it is blunt. Whereas an old knife, not even stainless steel, with a thin, rusty, well sharpened blade is in many cases the most valued tool in the kitchen.

You need at least one wooden spoon, and a wooden spatula is useful as well, since spoons don't always go into corners.

One of the best things about a wooden spoon is that you can taste soups without burning your tongue on the spoon. To avoid burning your tongue on the soup use the blow that God gave you.

They do of course harbour all sorts of germs, most of which are good for your immune system. But it is not a bad idea to scrub them well after use, and perhaps bleach them from time to time. There are various kinds and shapes. Don't go hog wild on buying them. They have a way of multiplying without too much help from you.

Another handy tool is a slice. They make them
in rubber or plastic for use with non-stick pans.
They also make them in stainless steel. These work
perfectly well with non-stick pans unless you use
them to scrape away burned bits.

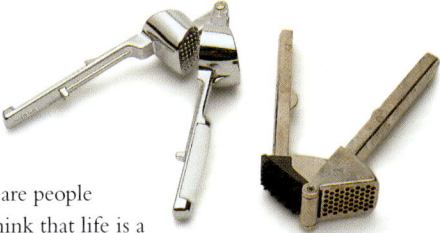

There are people
who think that life is a
barren desert if they have to
live without a garlic press. You may
end up being one of them. You may be one already.
My view is that most presses are more trouble than
they are worth, as they take so much cleaning. But
as the amount of taste you get from one clove of
garlic is roughly proportional to the smallness of the
pieces, the press, or a pestle and mortar, gets most
taste per clove.

   The only one I have now is the one you see with
a little black attachment. This, when you turn
the handles the other way, cleans the
bits of garlic out of the holes.
So earns its keep.

Garlic is sticky on
your hands and can be
difficult to unwrap. Another
gadget you can buy is a green
square in which you roll the clove
to loosen the skin.

You need a jug made
of fireproof glass which
is marked in litres, pints,
cups and anything else
that cooks and politicians
invent to confuse us.

Nowadays there are also some nice little sets like
little stainless steel saucepans that give you the
smaller measures, like tablespoons.

You will need a grater. There is always cheese
needing grating, and some people have been known
to eat grated carrots on salads without having a gun
held to their heads. It helps to have various degrees of
gratiness, since sooner or later someone

will want you to grate a nutmeg. Grated ginger improves many dishes, too.

Don't go mean on this. It won't be used every day, but a good one should see you out.

You can spend lots of money on scales for weighing. The modern ones will zero the measure when you have put the bowl on, so that it starts at nought as you add the sugar or the flour. But there is a lot to be said for the old-fashioned kind, cast iron, copper and a pleasure to have on a kitchen top. They are also easier to treat roughly, will not melt when accidentally exposed to heat and are scrubbable in the sink.

While we are on the subject of sinks, it is getting harder to find double sinks where the second rinsing sink hasn't become too small to be of much use to anybody. One of the solutions is to have bowls that you can fill. I regret that it makes most sense to use plastic ones. Although they get disgusting fairly soon, they can be easily replaced.

One day, when you feel you have earned it, and if you don't live without a garden, you can also get yourself a chopping board/bag combination, which allows you to sweep the discarded bits of vegetable in to the bag let into the kitchen top. The bag then gets emptied on to the compost heap in the garden.

You will want some of the various other tools we show, but you are better off buying them when you have a job for them to do, rather than building up drawers full of things that looked good but which you hardly ever use.

What you will need, of course, more than anything else is pans. There are many Rolls Royce owners, especially in France, who sell pans. And in due course you must be allowed to make your own extravagant mistakes. But to begin with it is wise to avoid aluminium. It seems there are a great many diseases that are rare in Africa, where iron pans are what people cook in. Connections have been established.

If you could buy only one pan, we would recommend a large cast iron one with a lid. No kitchen should be without one. It is important to keep detergents out of it, and to dress it lightly with oil to discourage rust.

A machined steel frying pan would also be your best bet if you could only afford two pans. Each of these will last you all your life, so long, that is, as you don't drop the cast iron one on a stone floor. Each can be used for a variety of uses.

If you can afford it we still think you should resist anything enamelled, and spend your money on stainless steel saucepans, the heavier the better.

They are easy to clean. Wire wool in getting rid of stubborn burns will only polish them brighter. Better to have only three heavy ones than five light ones. If in doubt go for size. You can cook anything in a large pan. There are far too many things that you can't fit into a small one.

You probably won't regret it if you let nothing into your kitchen made of plastic, even a washing up bowl.

What else is essential? No kitchen, in my view, should be without salt, pepper (black for seasoning, white for cooking), olive oil (extra virgin to eat raw, cheaper for cooking), butter, eggs, onions and garlic. Tins of tomatoes, and tins of sardines are useful stand-bys.

Bread is a staple. If you have been used to the stuff that feels like cotton wool, try some of the bread that has some weight to it. In some countries the bread is so good that you can eat it by itself, lovely hard crusts and chewy inside. But most of the bread sold today is neither nourishing nor good for you. Yet here, buy and eat what you like even if it doesn't do you any good. If you have tried other kinds and don't like them, leave them alone. There is no point in eating food you don't like eating.

Tools and how to use them

We'll start with the large knife. The sharper it is, the better it works. The sharper it is, the easier it will be to cut little bits off your fingers. It is thus very important to get into the habit of using the knife in the way that people have learned gives their fingers a longer life expectancy.

One of the first uses of the large knife is shredding greens, slicing cucumbers, anything where we are turning a sausage shape into slices.

With greens we begin by stripping out the stems with the small knife

and throwing the rest of the leaves into water. Then
we roll a bunch of them into a sausage shape and slice.

Notice that the part of the fingers nearest the knife
are the knuckles. The blade should never lift as high
as the knuckles and so there should be no danger to
the fingers.

If, as usually makes sense, you want then to make
some longways cuts keep your fingers on either side
of the knife blade.

The cucumber is a more advanced use of the same method. For sandwiches and salads the thinner the slices the more agreeable to eat. There are slicing machines, but if you learn to use the big knife you get pleasure from getting thin slices by your own hand. And you save washing up.

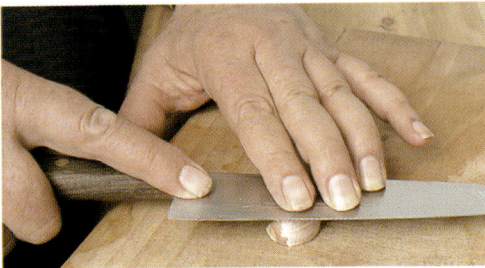

When they need garlic, professional cooks tend to lay their big knife on a clove and press down with their hand. You will hear a slight crack and the skin falls off more easily. On the other hand, if you use the small knife for chopping it up afterwards and don't want to clean two knives you can just as easily use anything lying around – a fairly full jar of jam, a weight from the scales, a full bottle of beer.

After that you can either cut daintily in both directions with the small knife,

or use the big one with the chopping motion so beloved of television cooks.

If all this seems too complicated, I notice that the blessed Jamie Oliver just gets on with it, topping and tailing his clove with the small knife. Then he peels. Then there is a little blur of chopping and the job is done.

In many parts of the world they peel potatoes with knives. Moreover they do so at great speed with minimum waste. In many cases they also take pleasure in removing the skin in the most niggardly fashion while still managing to keep it in one piece. Mind you, in most parts of the world the peel is neither thrown away nor composted. It is given to animals. Assuming you neither keep animals nor peel enough potatoes to make it worth developing these skills, a potato peeler is a good investment.

For a while there was some popularity in a kind of cylinder into which you threw the potatoes. Then you turned a handle and the potatoes tumbled about having the skin removed by various grating surfaces. On the whole these things took more storage space than they were worth, especially if they were big and electric, instead of being hand driven. It is easy to see that where there were eyes in the potatoes the eyes either remained in the potato and had to be removed by hand, or you had to continue grating until the amount of potato left to eat was a mere shadow of its former robust self.

Hand potato peelers are a different matter. Some people prefer fixed ones that don't swivel. My preference is for the swivel kind, and my favourite is the one with a big black handle. Since they are inexpensive it pays to try more than one kind. One will become your favourite. The others will do when you can't find where some idiot has put your favourite.

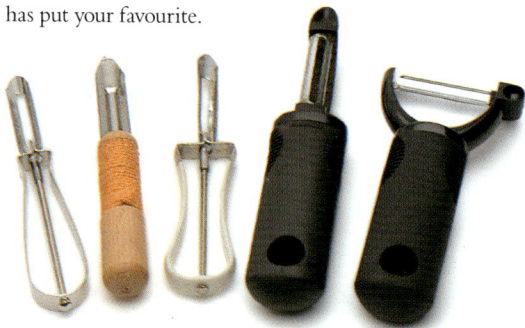

When we've got the peel off, there is always the chance that you will want to mash them. One way to turn your mashed potato into a kind of wallpaper paste is to give them to a blender. You would save washing up and achieve much the same result by buying potato powder. For a good result you need elbow grease. There are two tools.

The one that looks like a slice that has turned a corner is a good reliable tool. The same job is done by one that is oval shaped. My preference for the first is aesthetic, since it is all good strong stainless steel. One piece. The other is usually flimsier and more likely to rust or break, especially if it is, as they are so often are, at the cheap end of the market.

But now we also have one that I first saw being used by the 'two fat ladies' on their programme. It uses the garlic press principle, and does a more thorough job, since you have to lift all the potato pieces from the colander and put them into this. The ones above you usually work in the saucepan after the water has been drained and there is a tendency to think you are all done when in fact there may still be a lump or two tucked away in a corner of the pan.

There are several different kinds of tin openers. Turn up your nose at very few of them, since built in to all of them is a hiding gene, which they share with bottle openers and corkscrews. This ensures that when you can't finish cooking without the can of tomatoes the opener will have disappeared.

The most primitive opener is the kind that you rock, levering on the edge of the can, so that a blade does the cutting. They are even, happily, found on some penknives. Keep one of these.

The next kind, and most used, is the plier action that brings a roller and a ratchet into opposition. These seldom go wrong. But they don't open all cans. Tins of Campbells consommé, for example, seem often to have a meaner top, and the plier action doesn't close properly on them. Tins of sardines or corned beef, when as so often

happens the key supplied manages to break off the tongue, also don't yield too easily on the corners, which are tighter than the roller can handle. One of the advantages of this kind of opener is that you can actually hold the tin clear of the table while opening it.

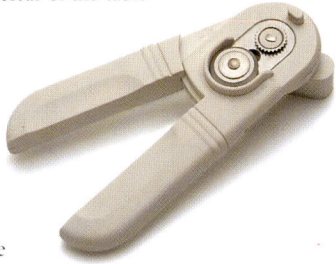

The next kind, which overcomes many of those problems with reluctant tins, cuts horizontally from the outside instead of vertically from inside the top. When you use it you may very occasionally spill liquids if the can is brimful. But these spills you can wipe up. It is always a pleasure to have some heavy artillery in the rear to crush opposition.

You can also, of course, move on to electric ones. Our advice is to wait until you really need one. There are always enough things wanting to get at your power points, and even more wanting to take space on your flat surfaces. Hand tin openers do neither. And tins should not be an important part of most cooking. How often can you fob yourself or the children off with baked beans on toast instead of something more like a balanced diet?

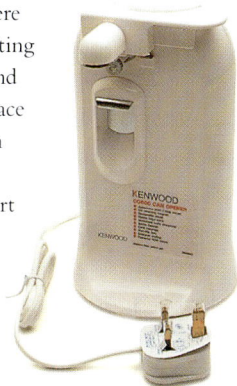

A colander isn't vital. You can always keep the vegetables back by holding the lid so that only liquid can run out. But it is a handsome and useful tool, so long as it isn't plastic, and is best hung on a hook over the sink, where it is easily reached.

There are other tools that aren't vital, a pretty sieve, a lemon squeezer, an egg whisk (which works rather better than a fork if you are in the habit of whisking things). Save buying them until you need to give yourself a treat.

Our last tool is a timer. You set it to a time, like four minutes, and it will tend to make an ugly noise when your time is up. Check the different noises before you part with any money.

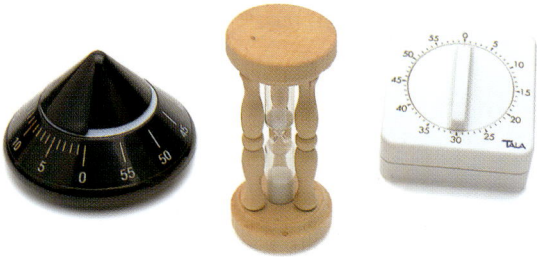

After that the tools are really gadgets. You can allow yourself one, a hand-held whizzer, simply because it is easy to clean and costs little, and is very useful for soups that use up the left-overs. That should do you, until you become involved in more complicated cooking, when you will know what you want next.

There will be a tool book in the series that you can buy if you want more toys in the kitchen. And which of us doesn't? But we have shown you enough to keep you going. One or two more, that have special jobs, will appear further into the book.

So now we can turn our attention to cooking.

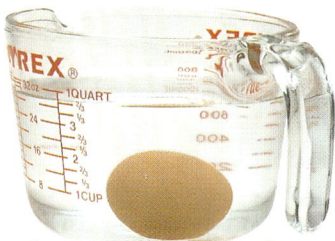

Things you probably know already

If you put an egg straight from the refrigerator into boiling water, the chances are it will crack. Keeping the eggs at room temperature reduces the chances of this happening. If it worries you then a pinprick to let the air out will limit the damage.

New laid eggs have rubbery shells, and can be thrown around without cracking. By the time they reach the shops their shells are brittle. But if you put the eggs into a saucepan of cold water you will learn a lot about the people who sold you your eggs. For the first day or two since laying the egg will lie on the bottom as though it was not in water.

Then as it gets older the unpointed end tends to lift, so that one end, instead of the middle, is on the bottom of the pan.

Gradually as days pass they get more upright. And finally, when they are only fit to throw away they will float.

The older they get the fewer ways there are to enjoy them. Hardboiled is best at the end of their lives, but one of the problems is that at the end of their lives the yolk has gone to one end and things like curried eggs may have only a very thin bit of white at one end.

Curried eggs are very easy to make, and do well for nibbles.

Peel the hardboiled eggs (8 minutes at least) by tapping the shells and then rolling them around until there are no large bits of shell. Then pop the shell off and cut the egg in half long ways.

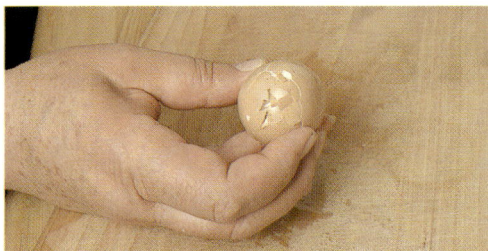

Remove the half yolks, mix them up with some mayonnaise, salt and curry powder to taste, and then pile the mixture back into the hole that the yolk came from in the first place.

It is worth doing the egg test until you find a shop that sells you reasonably fresh eggs, since poached eggs, soft boiled eggs and scrambled eggs taste far better when you use fresh eggs.

We should have started with onions, not eggs. But we might as well carry on. Everybody has a different rule about boiling eggs. One way is to put the egg(s) in cold water and when the water is genuinely boiling – none of these diffident bubbles beginning to appear – give them another full minute, and you will get solid white a d runny yolk.

Another way is to lower them gently into boiling water, and three and a half minutes will just give you solid white, while four makes the whole thing less marginal.

But you can work these times out for yourself, so that you know exactly how much your favourite egg takes. Remember, though, that half a dozen eggs in a little water will cool everything down and slow cooking down too. A single egg in a lot of boiling water, on the other hand, will tend to cook a little quicker.

It was for this reason that we included a timer among the tools. You generally would like to be laying a table, or toasting bread, instead of standing over a saucepan with a watch under your eye. The timer will call you when time is up.

More words have been written about scrambled eggs than have been written about the Magna Carta. Don't be intimidated. The only test is the eggs that you like the best, and the only way to discover this is to keep trying. You will save yourself a lot of pain, unless you like your scrambled eggs to have the texture of rubber, to remember always to cook slowly in a pan on very low heat.

Some people tell you to add milk. Others tell you to add water. What they call seminal writers like Eliza Acton didn't say anything about them, and it is possible that the first people to do so came after the war, perhaps Philip Harben, perhaps Elizabeth David. So start their way.

A decent whack of butter in a warm pan. Don't let the butter go brown. If it does you have warmed it too long or your heat is too high.

If you like to see flecks of white in your eggs don't beat them too much in the bowl. If you want all the same colour beat them a bit longer.

Added liquid speeds this along, but wait for adding liquid tests until you have tried cooking them as the hen laid them.

When the butter has melted add the mixture and gently stir it, just enough to stop one part cooking before another part.

Delia Smith likes you to keep some of the butter back and add it just before cooking has finished. I see no objection to this so long as it doesn't mean you are mean with the butter at the beginning. It is difficult, in my view, to over-butter scrambled eggs.

You can have added salt and pepper to the mixture. I prefer to do so afterwards, since black pepper shouldn't be cooked and black pepper is better than white for scrambled eggs.

Take the eggs off before they have become quite dry as they will continue cooking for a little while after they have left th pan.

Already you have lots of variations to try. On top of those you also have – beside the toast, or on the toast, cold toast or hot toast, heavy bread or fluffy bread, brown or white, buttered or not.

And when you have decided between all of those you can think in terms of adding bits of smoked salmon, which was a welcome after-theatre snack at the Garrick Club i London. Or tomato, or anything else that take your fancy.

Or go the whole hog. In Spain and South America they make their tortillas by adding most of the vegetable garden and other things, like sausage, besides. These are meals you know you've eaten when you have put one away.

Scrambled eggs is one of the best quick snacks you can make. It is worth taking the trouble to learn how to make the ones you like best.

Poached eggs support nearly the same amount of
literature and as many vehement opinions as does
the best way of washing up. There are now available
some egg poaching pans, usually a saucepan
that has within it four
non–stick little cups.

You put water in the bottom and put butter and salt
and pepper in as many of the cups as you expect to
use. The whole kit is usually too light for you to
crack the egg on the edge, so there is a tendency to
trail egg yolk across on your way to the cup. There is
also a tendency to burn your fingers when the eggs
are ready and you have to remove the cups.

Not to mention that, non–stick notwithstanding,
the cups don't clean easily. There are worse ways of
poaching eggs, but you would probably be wise to
try other ways before buying a pan that has only
one function. You will also earn Delia Smith's
approval.

Why not start with Eliza Acton, who says:

*'Take for this purpose a wide and delicately clean pan
about half-filled with the clearest spring water; throw in
a small spoonful of salt, and place it over a fire quite free
from smoke. Break some new laid eggs into separate cups,
and do this with care, that the yolks may not be injured.*

When the water boils draw back the pan, glide the eggs

gently into it, and let them stand until the whites appear almost set, which will be in about a minute: then, without shaking them, move the pan over the fire and just simmer them for two and a half to three minutes. Lift them out separately with a slice, quickly trim off the ragged edges and serve them.

Serve them upon dressed spinach, or upon minced veal, turkey or chicken; or dish them for an invalid upon delicately toasted bread, sliced thick, and freed from crust; it is an improvement to have the bread buttered but it is then less wholesome.'

Some people used to recommend a little vinegar instead of salt. Many don't remove the pan. Some stir the water into a circle and drop the egg in the middle to theoretically limit the spread of the yolk.

New laid eggs are the important thing. Old eggs don't get younger when they are poached.

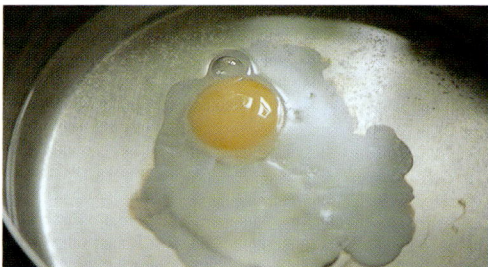

That leaves us with only fried eggs standing between you and the onions. You will have to wait for the egg book to learn about coddled eggs and all the other things that can be done. Fried eggs again need a warm pan. You don't want it too hot. You want enough fat to allow you to lift the egg without breaking it, or to turn it over for those people who don't like to see a yellow yolk.

Now onions.

They range in appearance and
strength from large and white to small and brown,
and from a strong taste down to the Walla Walla
onions. These (originating from the south eastern
United States, but stolen and promoted in the state
of Washington) are so mild that Californian banks
pile them up in their foyer in season, and people
take them and eat them like apples.

The fresher onions are the firmer they will be. The
stronger tasting are the yellow ones. Red varieties
vary in taste, and white ones tend to be the mildest.

The more used a country is to fast food the less
they use shallots. The French have better sense.
Because they are smaller you have to prepare more
to get the same volume. But the taste is worth the
trouble, especially in stews and suchlike.

Scallions and spring onions are usually eaten raw
or very lightly cooked in a stir-fry. They give a lift
to any salad. You don't want to be obsessive about
washing everything you eat, although it only does
good; but it is proper to wash these fairly thoroughly before eating them since they are usually grown
in places where all sorts of involuntary additives can
arrive and cling to the skin.

You will find nobody who approves of how you prepare an onion. Some will tell you to do it under water to save the tears. Most professional cooks nowadays follow the Received view, which is to cut the onion in half and keep the stem intact to hold on to. Then you cut in the other direction.

If you haven't gone into your hand because your knife was not sharp enough and you were therefore pressing too hard, you will have a chopped onion.

If you can't be bothered with all that palaver, those nice Dorling Kindersley books tell you to cut the onion in half from the stem end to the root end.

Then with the flat side down on the board you hold
the root end and cut away from your hand in slices
of the appropriate thickness.

Then you turn the onion through ninety degrees
and cut in the other direction.

If you can't even be bothered with that, start by
cutting off the two ends. Then stand the onion on
the board with one of the cut ends on top and the
other on the board and cut in half.

Then you peel off the skin. If the onion is getting
on in age it will be softer than it should be, and one

of the layers of skin near the outside will be thin and slimy. Get down to this in your peeling and get rid of it, since it adds nothing to your cooking and it tends to encourage the knife to slip.

Then you just cut in slices in one way, and move your hand and the knife, but not the onion, and cut in the other direction.

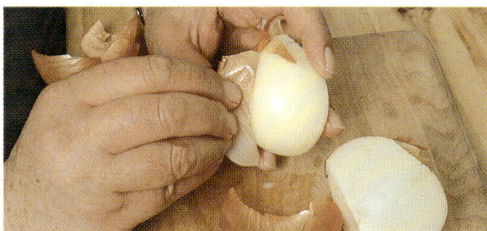

Remember to hold the last bit with your fingers bent so that you don't risk any cuts.

There is no limit to the improvements onions can make to food. There is, for example, a delicious rice dish using only onions and butter, salt and pepper. A stew built without onions is rather like an engine without fuel.

The best known vegetable on the fringes of the onion family is the leek, and one of the best uses you can put it to is with leek and potato soup.

Leeks are not that easy to clean, since earth tends to lodge between layers. Mostly the earth is near the top and near the outside. The best way to solve this is to cut off the root, and the bits at the top that look too manky to bring people hurrying to eat them. Strip off dreary looking outside layers, which you will have if the leeks have been lying around too long. Then split them lengthways.

Some people suggest you then swish these halves around in water. Bearing in mind that the leeks are going to be boiled, and that earth left behind will both be sterilised and sink to the bottom of the pan, there is nothing wrong with this. But it is no real

hardship to strip off the outside layers and throw
them into a large bowl of water until you see no
more earth, and you are left with a clean core.

Then you can chop up the core and gather the outer leaves from the bowl, shake off the water and chop them up as well.

Now you've got them clean you might as well make the soup. Put a couple of leeks chopped into some olive oil in a pan and cook them until they become transparent. This is called blanching in a lot of books, and is a good start for most dishes using leeks and onions.

Peel one large potato or a couple of small ones. Chop up the potato. If you have stock use it. Otherwise add a cube of vegetable or even chicken stock to some boiling water and add the potatoes. This will make a bowl for at least four people, so the liquid should have the leek and potatoes sloshing around. Add salt and white pepper. When the potatoes have become soft, the soup is ready.

You can use a potato masher to break it up a bit. Or you can use the electric whizzer that we let you buy to make it creamy. If you used too little water you can add milk. If you used too much let the whole thing simmer a while until some of the water has evaporated.

One of the cheapest, easiest and most delicious soups you can make. Students who waste what little money they have on junk food would do well to remember this.

More nourishing.

Less expensive.

Tastier.

What next?

Sooner or later you will be asked to make a roux. Even if you are not you should know how because of all those dishes that need white sauce. Other dishes like macaroni cheese also start with a roux.

It is a French word. It is pronounced Roo (like the baby Kanga carried around in Winnie the Pooh), and it is one of those OK words that cooks like to use. It is also one of the more important building blocks of a great many dishes that are really worth knowing how to cook.

Put simply, you add sifted flour very slowly to melted butter, stirring as you add it. The proportions used to be seven ounces of flour to half a pound of butter. Thus a little less flour than there was butter in weight. As butter now tends to come in packs of 250 grams, you will want about 210 grams of flour. Half of each if you want less.

The trick is to use a low heat and to sift and add the flour slowly enough not to have a lump problem. Roux never looks that appealing, just a dryish mixture of butter and flour. But you can put it into a jar and draw from it for several days.

Roux was used for thickening things, and people get very ritzy about how it should be made. But I saw a well known cook in New Orleans pour what looked like a pint of oil into a pan, heat it, and casually add a whole load of flour to make a brown roux. It looked fine, and they tell me that the stew it was added to was marvellous.

For brown roux you heat the butter a little longer, by the way. One of the most common uses of roux is to make a white sauce to put over vegetables. This is more fun to make.

You have it all in the pan, but the flour won't be cooked yet. It will never be cooked until you add it to whatever you want to thicken.

Making the white sauce you gradually add milk, still stirring, and your mess will bubble away if you don't add the milk too quickly. All the while the flour will be cooking. Continue until you have a white sauce that you can pour. Add salt to taste. This, too, will keep.

For macaroni cheese you take the heated white sauce when it is still fairly thick and drop in little lumps of a nice strong cheese. If you grate the cheese it will melt even quicker.

What could be simpler than to be boiling some macaroni in a pot while you are making the cheese sauce? Then you drain the water, pop the macaroni into a heat-proof bowl, pour on the sauce, add some pepper and put it under the grill for a few minutes to brown the top.

Add a salad and you have another quick tasty meal. Which brings us on to salad and salad dressing.

Salad vegetables

Nowadays there seem to be hardly any vegetables that somebody doesn't prefer raw. Yet we should start with the ones we use most often, lettuce and other greenery, tomatoes, scallions (spring onions), what we call chicory and what the French call endive, and watercress.

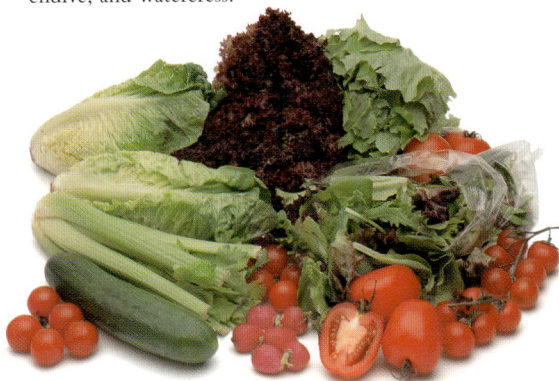

You want to be careful here, because supermarkets have gone in for packaging salad mixes, and some of them are three or four times the price you would pay if you bought the ingredients separately.

Salads can get very complicated, as can also the dressings for salads. You can buy salad dressings, but there are none you can buy that are as good as what you can make yourself. Some people, particularly Americans, like a sweet taste in their dressing. You won't find it difficult to search out recipes for salad dressing, yet here again we recommend that you start with the basic minimum: salt, pepper, oil and vinegar or lemon. Since there is also a choice of vinegars, start with lemon.

Take a crisp lettuce, wash the leaves well, and cut it into fine shreds. Add, if you like, some tomatoes, so long as they are reasonably ripe and tasty, also sliced small. Put the whole lot in a large bowl. Add salt and pepper and 'extra virgin' olive oil. What on earth is an extra virgin?

Then roll a couple of lemons around so that the insides have taken a bit of a battering. Cut them open and squeeze them on to the salad, tossing and mixing the salad as you do it, so that you can stop adding lemon, or add any of the other ingredients to taste.

This can be your bench mark. You can then another time try adding other ingredients like mustard to your dressing, and other ingredients like spring onions or broccoli or even peppers to your salad.

Cooking vegetables

The reason many people don't eat enough vegetables is because so often they are well past sell-by date when they reach the home, and they are cooked without care and attention. Nobody enjoys eating the result. In many cases too, because of this, you will find that frozen vegetables taste better and cost less than what are laughingly called fresh vegetables. Broad beans are a very good example, splendid frozen, seldom even interesting in the pod.

Ideally vegetables should be steamed instead of boiled, simply because no taste is leached into the boiling water when they are steamed. But since at this stage we haven't included a steamer among your kitchen basics, you can overcome the problem by using only as much water as will last until the vegetables are done. Just before the pan might begin to burn, if you have timed it right, you can tip out the vegetables and only a drop or two of water will be left.

Don't get locked into the idea that water is the only way you can cook vegetables. There are lots of opportunities in the oven as well.

Protein

There isn't enough space to go too deeply into how to cook protein in this little book. The most popular meat seems to be chicken, despite the fact that the poor little things are fed such rubbish that they end up pale and tasteless. A chicken that has led a normal life, eating normal food, has yellow flesh, and tastes of chicken. What you can buy these days hasn't these advantages, so that you have to find other ways of making it taste of something.

Grilling works quite well. Roasting works better, since you can add flavour. Alternatively you can stew them with onions and use them in a stew, or in a rice dish.

Chops of beef, lamb or pork are most often either grilled or fried. Yet going for bigger cuts and roasting them is often less trouble. There was a time when Sundays involved preparing the potatoes and vegetables, and then putting the joint of meat and the potatoes in the oven. Then you went to church. When you got back you took some of the juice for making gravy, you basted the joint, and you put the vegetables on. If you were energetic you also made some white sauce for the leeks or onions. Then, by the time the vegetables were ready the table would be laid, and you could all sit down to the family meal. This still makes a hard act for any pub to follow on a Sunday, both for taste and price.

Fish is another very good food that has largely fallen out of favour, except in the Mediterranean countries. In Seattle, where they fondly believe they have the best fish in the world, the choice is largely limited to dead oysters, farmed salmon, halibut, and one or two others brought in from places like Hawaii.

Whereas even in the middle of France you will find live oysters at affordable prices, not to mention fish like grey and red mullet and many others, that do not look or taste as though they have been on the slab for the last eleven days. In Britain there has been a tendency to go for the white fish that have less of a bone problem.

But it is encouraging that both mackerel and herring are coming back to the supermarkets. A grilled mackerel, albeit usually far older than it should have been, is still the easiest fish to cook under the grill, and the easiest to detach from its bones.

For the best nourishment at the lowest price you have to investigate stews. You can stew any meat, including fish, and the cheapest cuts often make the best stew. Potatoes, onions, salt and pepper and oil with meat of some kind is, again, all you need.

Not that you can't add anything else that takes your fancy. If turnips or swedes or parsnips are cheap, use them instead of potatoes. Cheap greens, slightly over the hill, will also work. Remember that all the great dishes, like Irish stew, were made by giving careful attention to how to make the best use of the cheapest ingredients. This was the problem that most people had to face. It is particularly interesting, for example, that it is hard now to make Irish stew, simply because you can't buy mutton. It is not nearly as good made with lamb.

Herbs

Angelica: Salads, custards, tart fruit (rhubarb, greengages) and in court bouillon.

Basil: Use with meat, fish, salads, stews, soups, and any combination with tomatoes.

Bay: Stews, soups, fish, stock and in bouquet garni.

Bergamot: Summer drinks, herb teas, salads and added to vegetable dishes.

Borage: Pimms No 1, or finely chopped with buttered vegetables.

Burnet: Cold chicken, seafood and white wine cups all benefit from fresh sprigs.

Chervil: Poached fish, omelettes and scrambled eggs, chicken, garnish, and soups, stews, and salads.

Chives: Use chopped raw with eggs, salads, sauces and soups. The flowers, too, are good in salad.

Coriander: Fish, curries, soups, stir fries, and with chutneys and relishes.

Cumin: In hot dishes, like chilli and curry. Also works with cabbage and Mrs Copty's lentil and pasta dish.

Dill: Herring, salmon, seafood, omelettes, cold soups, stuffed vine leaves, pickling, salad and salad dressing.

Fennel: the chopped leaves with fish. The seeds in bread. The plant itself is also marvellous poached with tomato and garlic.

Hyssop: Dried leaves are good in soups and teas. Fresh leaves in sandwiches and pasta dishes. Flowers for salads if you want to deprive the butterflies, for whom the bush is worth planting.

Lemon Balm: Omelettes and egg dishes, herbal teas and anything else that takes your bored fancy.

Lemon Grass: In Thai curries and soups, particularly with chicken and seafood. Beware of stabbing yourself.

Lemon Verbena: Add to fresh fruit drinks and herb teas.

Lovage: Soups, salads, stuffings, stews, and meat dishes.

Marjoram: Soups, stews and stuffings, pizzas, and pastas.

Mint: Soups, salads, sauces, confectionery, and herbal teas.

Oregano: This is a form of marjoram, specially good in pasta or beef dishes.

Parsley: Cooked vegetables, generously; and as a garnish.

Rosemary: A must almost with lamb, and use sparingly in salads, sauces, stews.

Saffron: Very slight flavour, very expensive, colours risotto and cakes.

Sage: Good with all meat dishes, specially pork, and stuffings, salads or spreads.

Savory: Blends well, meat
stuffings, vegetable soups, beans,
fish, eggs, poultry, and sausages. ▶

◀ **Sorrel**: A sour taste, lovely in
mixed salads and sandwiches.

Sweet Cicely: Puddings made with
ice cream and/or fruit, whipped
cream, and rice pudding.

Tansy: Finely chopped for
salads, omelettes, custards
cakes, minced meat. ▶

◀ **Tarragon**: Fish, omelettes,
poultry, mushroom, salads,
stews, and with sauces like
Bearnaise and tartare.

Thyme: Soups, stuffings,
meats, fish, and sauces. ▶

◀ **Turmeric**: Bean and lentil
dishes, kedgeree, and found
in curry powders.

Measurements

Measurements are a mess. You have to cope with the fact that in North America they have 16 fluid ounces to a pint, while in England there are 20. This is one of the reasons why a gallon of petrol in England has more liquid than a gallon of gasoline in America.

Since you may be shown recipes in old books, in American books and even in continental books you will find proportions in any of these. It won't be the end of the world if you use 150 grams instead of 171 for 6 ounces. Nor will it come to an end if you are using an English pint in an American cook book, although it may end up wetter than was intended. The safest course is to convert to the measures that you can measure.

One pound is 0.45359 kilograms, or 453.59 grams.
UK pint is 4 gills and is 568.3 millilitres.
1 US pint, which is also 4 gills, is 473.6 millilitres.
In America a cup is equal to half a North American pint in liquid.

Broadly speaking it may help to remember that two cups weigh around a pound of things like rice or lentils. Thus, if an American recipe calls for four cups of sugar you will probably want to have a two pound bag handy.

Litres and kilograms are meant to sustain the idea that a litre of water weighs a kilogram, and occupies a thousand cubic centimetres, which it more or less does. So perhaps the only thing to cling to, if you are having to deal with cups of liquid, is that 4 cups are a little under a litre [947 instead of a thousand].

1 kilogram is 2.20462 lbs.
1 litre is 1.7598 UK pints.

1 UK fluid oz is a twentieth of 568.3 millilitres or 28.415 millilitres.
1 American fluid ounce is one sixteenth of 473.6 or 29.6 millilitres.

If we haven't confused you by now you are exceptional. Don't worry about it. We will give you tables in the end papers which may help. You can also devise any conversion you want from the information above. But in general the main problem is proportions not exact amounts and these will come with practice.

Few people need to measure five tablespoons of olive oil if they are not working in a pharmacy. You are more likely to think in terms of a large dollop. And then you taste it. If it is too little you add a small dollop. If it is too much you remember next time that you want to go a little lighter on the dollop.

In many cases the exact amount is irrelevant. For example, a good way of cooking rice is to cook some onions in olive oil or butter until they look transparent. Then you can take any old mug from the kitchen and fill it with rice and dump it in the pan, stirring it around until the fat has soaked into the rice. Then add twice as much boiling water or stock, season and stir it until it is boiling again.

Then you turn the heat right down, put a lid on it and leave it alone. After about twenty minutes the liquid will have been absorbed by the rice, and you will have finished your gin, made a salad and laid the table, and the rice will be ready to eat.

You could also have added anything else, like tomatoes, prawns, bits of chicken, parmesan cheese, green or red peppers for colour or anything else that took you fancy. The grams and millilitres didn't come into it. The only thing that mattered is that even a small mug of rice feeds at least two people. Just as 150 grams of pasta is needed for a reasonably hungry person. Since pasta usually comes in packs of 500 grams you don't really care that this is a little more than a pound, and a 150 gram helping is around five ounces.

These are the things you will discover, and which you will need to remember.

Glossary

of some of the words they throw at you

Au gratin: a dish with cheese or other sauce or breadcrumbs or any mixture thereof and then browned under the grill, or in the oven.

Basting: moistening the upside of roasting food to stop it getting too dry. A necessity, really, with roast potatoes and birds and joints of meat, to get that crisp finish.

Béchamel: a flavoured white sauce named after a steward of the French king Louis XIV.

Blanch: to cover in boiling water and leave to soak for a few minutes.

Braise: strictly this only means to stew in a closed vessel, but in the kitchen we expect to brown the food, usually in a very hot pan, first.

Bouquet garni: a bunch or little bag of herbs to season a stew, but which can be removed before serving. Usually contains parsley, thyme and bay leaf.

Fines herbes: the traditional four horsemen of chives, parsley, tarragon and chervil. To test the skill of a chef ask for an omelette fines herbes. Only too often in a so-called fancy restaurant it comes out like what at school we used to call 'wet dog'. But don't confuse 'wet dog' which was the best you could get out of powdered egg, with 'baveuse', which is how many of us like our omelettes, slightly moist like the tongue of a dog.

Croutons: little deep fried cubes of bread that are scattered on soups, and which also turn a Caesar salad into a calorific nightmare.

Marinade: a usually acidic liquid mixture, that may include wine, vinegar or lemon juice, in which you can soak meats and fish to improve their flavour and soften them up for people who like food you can eat with your gums.

Parboil: this actually means to boil thoroughly, but as happens with many words these days, especially when talking about computers, an entirely wrong meaning has also become current. Many if not most people think it means part boiled. They talk of parboiling potatoes before roasting them. They almost certainly mean part boiling.

Sauté: some of us used to claim that this referred to food that was fried after it had been part boiled. The world tells us we were wrong and it means fried lightly and quickly. We thought that was stir-fry.

Scalding: this usually means burning yourself with a hot liquid. In cooking it means to bring something to just below the boil. Milk, for instance, is better scalded than boiled.

Postscript

There are a million things that might have been in this book, and even we couldn't agree about what to include. In general we have tried to say what so many cookery books assume people know, but not all of us have picked up.

The conversion tables that are such a necessity for the many people who use recipes from other countries we have put in the end papers, where they are easier to find if you have hands covered in flour. It is probably also helpful to be able to sort out some of the more common disasters.

Burnt pans

There may be no substitute for elbow grease, tempting as it is to leave them to soak in the hope that either the burn will become softer or that somebody else will do the job.

Covering the burnt parts with plenty of water, and adding a lot of salt, boiling, and leaving to stand overnight is said to help. We certainly do it from time to time, but suspect that it only seems easier because one is usually less tired in the morning.

If you have gone in for non-stick, on the other hand, elbow grease will probably take much of the non-stick with the burn. If it doesn't come off easily, throw the pan away and buy a heavy one of stainless or iron, that likes being scratched with wire wool.

Too much salt

Cream helps in a soup. Dilution is the real answer. Add more liquid or more vegetables, or both.

Or throw it away and start again to avoid having some parts overcooked, or other parts undercooked.

Too much fat

Let it come to the top and mop it up with paper towels or tissues. One of those basting syringes can also be used. Or get it cold enough to lift it off with a spoon.

To revive stale bread

Run water over the loaf and put it in a moderate (say 375 or gas 4) oven for ten or fifteen minutes. It will look and taste as though it was just baked. You can steam a stale cake for rather longer and it will also seem as though it was just baked.

For standby

A sliced loaf in the freezer, if you have one, is a good standard. You can then toast the slices you need in the toaster, if you have one, and not have to worry about waste or going stale. Long life milk, horrid as it is, is also worth keeping for emergencies. Spare butter in the freezer can earn its keep as well. While we are at the freezer, there are many vegetables (peas, broad beans, sliced runner beans) that are usually better bought frozen than what is laughingly called fresh. Frozen summer fruits like raspberries and currants are also good, (especially heated and eaten with vanilla ice cream) and usually much less expensive.

Bibliography

There are more cookbooks than anybody can ever read. These are favourites:

Eliza Acton: Modern cookery for Private Families, first published in 1845 and called by Elizabeth David, another person whose books you should read, 'the greatest cookery book in our language'.

Mrs Beeton: Household Management. Mrs Beeton was not as good looking as Susanna Whatman, and her book is longer and seems as out of place in the later twentieth century, but it is still as valuable a possession as you can find on a kitchen bookshelf.

Fanny Farmer's Boston Cooking School Cookbook

Philip Harben: Cooking, and The Grammar of Cookery

Cook's Ingredients: Dorling Kindersley Pocket Encyclopedia

The Joy of Cooking

The Cookery Year, Readers Digest Association Ltd, a reliable old standby

Delia Smith: The Complete Cookery Year, published by the BBC

Jane Grigson's Vegetable Book, is all you can possibly remember about ways to cook vegetables

Elizabeth David: French Provincial Cooking (or any other)

Herbs

	Meat	Poultry	Fish	Soups & Stews	Salads	Sauces	Eggs	Pastas
Angelica					●			
Basil	●		●	●	●	●		●
Bay			●	●		●		
Bergamot					●			
Burnet		●	●					
Chervil		●	●	●	●	●	●	●
Chives				●	●	●	●	
Coriander			●	●		●		
Dill			●	●	●		●	
Fennel			●					
Hyssop					●			●
Lemon Balm							●	
Lemon Grass		●	●	●				